salmonpoetry
Diverse Voices from Ireland and the World

Sketch of Michael G. Casey by Peter Fitzgerald

Broken Circle
Michael G. Casey

Published in 2023 by
Salmon Poetry
Cliffs of Moher, County Clare, Ireland
Website: www.salmonpoetry.com
Email: info@salmonpoetry.com

Copyright © Michael G. Casey, 2024

ISBN 978-1-915022-41-7

All rights reserved. No part of this publication may be reproduced or transmitted in any form or by any means, electronic or mechanical, including photography, recording, or any information storage or retrieval system, without permission in writing from the publisher. The book is sold subject to the condition that it shall not, by way of trade or otherwise, be lent, resold or otherwise circulated without the publisher's prior consent in any form of binding or cover other than that in which it is published and without a similar condition, including this condition, being imposed on the subsequent purchaser.

Cover Image: *'The Broighter Collar'* © *National Museum of Ireland*
Page 1: *Sketch of Michael G. Casey by Peter Fitzgerald*
Cover Design & Typesetting: *Siobhán Hutson Jeanotte*

Printed in Ireland by Sprint Print

Salmon Poetry gratefully acknowledges the support of
The Arts Council / An Chomhairle Ealaíon

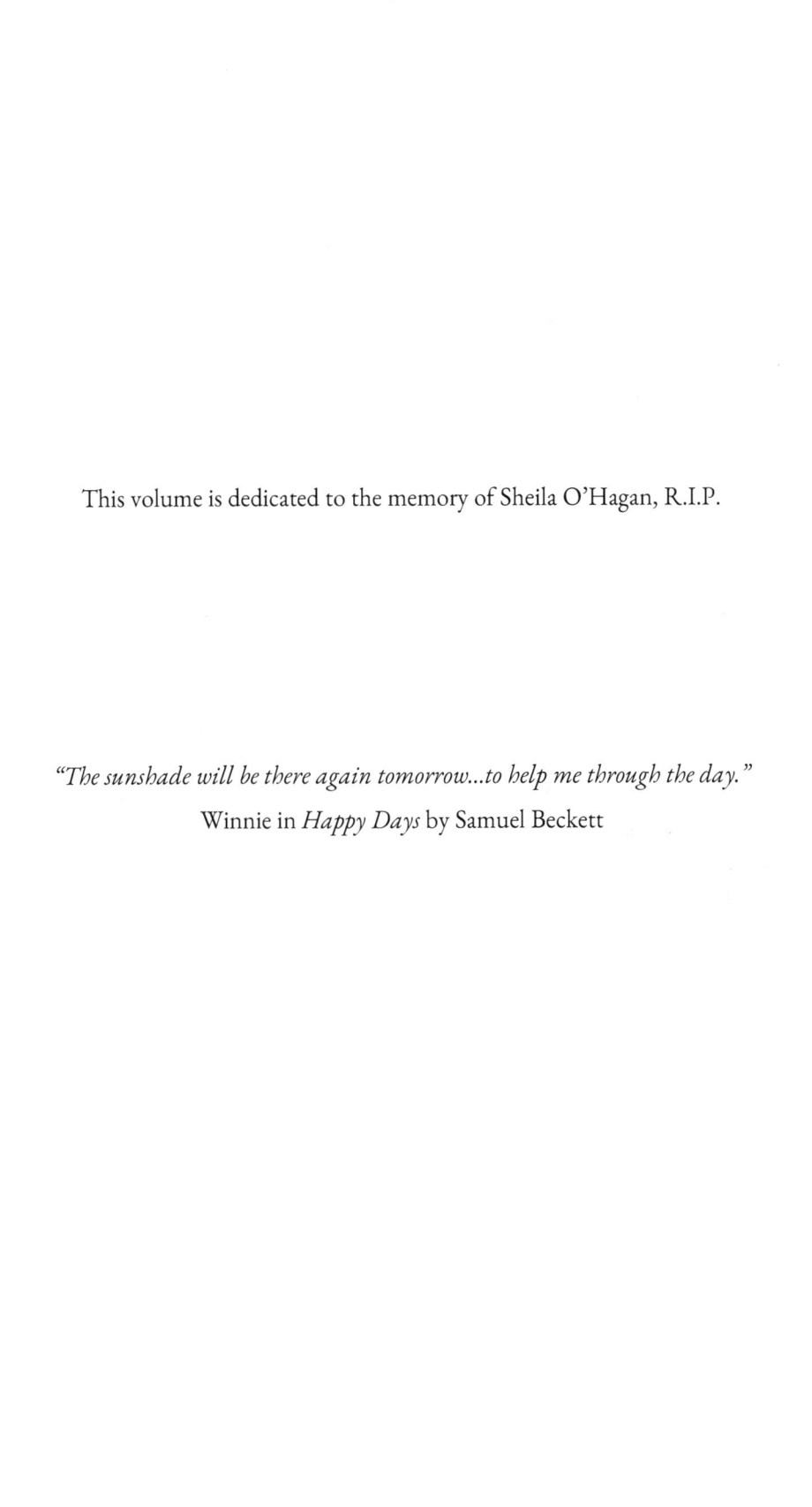

This volume is dedicated to the memory of Sheila O'Hagan, R.I.P.

"The sunshade will be there again tomorrow...to help me through the day."
Winnie in *Happy Days* by Samuel Beckett

Contents

FLIGHT	11
THE LOSS THAT HEIGHT ENTAILS	13
BIRDS OF SALT AIR	14
AN EXALTATION OF LARKS	15
THE SEA'S UNCERTAINTY	16
GEOLOGISTS AND PARABLES OF EARTH	17
A LADYBIRD'S JOURNEY ACROSS A LEAF	18
BULLOCH HARBOUR, WINTER 2017	20
CLOUDS CEASE DRIFTING	21
MY CAT'S X-RAY	22
THE SHAPE OF RAIN	23
MOUSE THROW	24
FLUKE	25
TOUCH	26
A PAIR OF CODGERS	28
FEELING THE ECLIPSE	30
THE CORMORANT FISHING COMPANY	31
THE TRINITY CAT	32
ANOTHER PRESENCE	33
MR. PHOTON	34
NOSTOS	35
THE CLIMBER THINKS OF HOME	36
SANDMAN'S LULLABY	37
WAITING WITH A VIEW OF THE LANE	38
GOING HOME THAT NOVEMBER	39
A MANDOLIN HUNG IN THE SHED	40
A PLANE AT NIGHT	42
RECOGNITION	43
JUST MARBLES	44
WATER PLAY	45
THE STILL CENTRE	47

ANCIENT ENTERTAINMENT	48
A FATE TAKES A HOLIDAY	50
GOLD OR GRAIL	52
THE HORSEMAN DREAM	53
A SPLINTER OF LIGHT	54
FASHION (OR ZEITGEIST?)	55
COMA	56
SUCH CLOSENESS	57
I WAS A FROZEN EMBRYO	58
RICHLY IMPRESSIVE THEN	59
BROKEN CIRCLE	60
LEAVENED BREAD	61
TOLSTOY'S MYRIAD LANDSCAPES	62
SNAPSHOT AND WAFFLES	64
WHERE IS THE GUIDE?	66
GIVERNEY AND OTHER GARDENS	67
GUITAR IN SHOP WINDOW	68
ENGLISH SPEAKS SEDUCTIVELY	69
ARBONAUTS IN A GONDOLA	71
BRISE-SOLEIL	72
LOVE POEM	73
SWIMMING TO ICELAND	74
I KNOW THE SCORE	76
BACK TO THE WORLD	77
ALWAYS IN SEARCH	78
Acknowledgements	81
About the author	82

FLIGHT

My arms grew beyond their normal length;
bones at the leading edge were light
and pared to cleaving rims; from these
came major spurs which put out
softer quills and ribs, patterned like
the veins of leaves but overlaying
each other, layered and flocculent,
in fantail and dovetail, proportioned
to the spheres for flexibility and grace.

Coverts fully formed and spread
to catch the morning, I felt the breeze
lift like a miracle and I gently
moved off the cliff, entering seamlessly
the new element of air; at first I fell
and the wind rushed past at suicidal speed,
killing all illusion, but instinct leapt to protect.
My descent was slowed by spread canopies
and, buoyed by thermals, I rose in the vaunt
and, gradually—true to my new nature—
drifted even higher and learned to glide.

With less effort than a sigh I lay
and floated on the gifted air.
My wings scarcely moved and then serenely,
mantles filled by up-draughts,
rising skywards over fields of grain.
Even the wispiest barbule knew its purpose
and could foil the smallest ruffle,
resist the occasional downward pull.

As air cooled over sea I used my wings
more energetically until the vanes were sleek
and flossed and could keep perfect time.
I could feel space, and sense, by taste
and sight, the versatility of air and light.
I learnt quickly on the wing and saw the universe.

I had grown into my desire and hovered for a while,
lying on the currents, marking time,
wanting more than had been given;
and then I swooped.

THE LOSS THAT HEIGHT ENTAILS

Icarus kept running in and out
with little feathers for his father.
Will these do, Daddy? These ones?

This was the memory that haunted
Daedalus as he pretended to listen
to his precocious nephew Perdix

spouting ideas of science
as if nothing had happened,
as if theory could be trusted.

That prick never knew the meaning
of excitement, never took a risk
and yet he had already invented

the saw (based on a cuttle fish spine
that had accidentally cut his hand.)
Strange that one without a soul

should have such luck.
Inventions notwithstanding,
the wrong one had survived.

Daedalus should have had
a better knowledge of the gods
for when he pushed Perdix

off a cliff they intervened, for
reasons known only to themselves,
and turned that unworthy youth

into a partridge, a bird that ever since,
despite the perfection of its wings,
makes its nest in low-lying places.

BIRDS OF SALT AIR

White and grey puff-ball seabirds
perched on the harbour wall,
face into gales, and shift orange feet
to find new balance after buffeting gusts.

Wind flows around bills and heads,
narrow and sleek, ruffles main feathers
and sends shivers along new downy fluff.
Fulmars sway to the music of air;

unflustered by storm, they groom
breast plumage, and manoeuvre necks
to reach wing-tip feathers. A white tern
trips along on pipe-cleaner legs

with knees like knots in thread, uses
salt wind to dry fantail wings.
A powerful squall induces them
to abandon positions and yield

gracefully to soaring instincts,
angle themselves for lift, and allow
superior elements raise them up,
fluttering and tilting, on capricious air,

not fussed at all about the challenge
of making headway against such force,
or the precise feathered adjustments
needed to survive the eye of storms.

AN EXALTATION OF LARKS

A wondrous word that lies in state
in the catafalque of language;
by what surge of spirit was it coined,
those four pure notes of perfect pitch,
soaring to the sight of morning birds
in breathless air, a psalm worthy
of its theme? It must have been
the rapture of a child, heedless
of rules, who brought awakening
hope to the verge of metaphor.

THE SEA'S UNCERTAINTY

Every sailor knew that Ursa Minor
contained the pole star;
they knew how to cope with gales,
smear their canvas clothes with tar
to keep the elements at bay, trim the sails.

They could fathom the semaphore
of swooping gulls, the cry and pitch
of curlews, horizon anchor-light,
the breaching of sea mammals,
sudden sounds in the cave of night.

But they feared uncertainty, sights
beyond telling at sea or ashore;
old shellbacks who saw much
more than younger men, were known to
go below to pray in creaking holds,
especially when an albatross brought
them their dead friends souls.

The ship a church, and figurehead
a sacred being with all-seeing eyes
to find the way. Athena's breasts
once calmed the storms, scattered
sirens and put out Elmo's fire.

Neptune driving a pair of seahorses
settled them, or Jupiter astride his eagle.
Sometimes an animal's head
under the bowsprit would suffice.
Any carving could become a god.
A silver coin in the keel gave hope,
a gold coin beneath the mast.

GEOLOGISTS AND THE PARABLES OF EARTH

The world is their oyster, especially in fossil form;
in jeans and open sandals they travel to the ends of earth
with silver hammers and poacher satchels of scuffed leather.

They chip away at sedimentary time, read waves of strata
like music scores, search for recurring phrases,
tap into grooved archives for stories that may become epics.

See them squatting on haunches in rust-coloured canyons
or on the blue Himalayan plains, poring over lapidary tales
whose endings are light years away and can't be explained.

Rocks do not volunteer to speak the psalm of language or offer
up their secrets easily, and we must be grateful
to these grizzled men who inspect the earth, prospecting,
not for gold, but for the scripture of ancient stone.

A LADYBIRD'S JOURNEY ACROSS A LEAF

With injured wings I hastened
across the green plains of the lamina
towards the ridge of the main stalk;
an instinct made me cross that divide
to see and explore the other side;
maybe it was a matter of survival.

I doubted if any unwary green-fly
would cross my path, and I had to be
on the alert against vicious attacks
from orange talons and beaks;
my lustrous carapace of red and black
hardly made me inconspicuous.

As I travelled on, fatigue set in
and then the realisation grew
that the ridge I hastened to
might merely be a rib or bundle
of veins and not the central
dividing line I had to reach.

I was lost in immense green space,
bewildered by repeating patterns
and the promise of further complexity.
I even worried for a while that this leaf
might be insectivorous, and mistook
some nearby hollows for stomata.

A breeze came up and I had to rest
for a while in the dorsal skin,
trying not to sink too far in.
I had to eat part of the venation
but, not wishing to harm the leaf,
made sure not to pierce the cuticle.

It was nightfall when I finally reached
what seemed to be the watershed stalk,
though it could have been yet another rib.
I rested in its lee and, fearing disappointment,
decided not to cross over until morning.

BULLOCH HARBOUR, WINTER 2017

Several apostolic fishing boats shaped
like eucalyptus leaves, curving up to bows,
all heaving side by side, catenaries
keen to slice through swollen seas beyond the walls.

But no one's going out in force-eight gales
oarlocks are removed from gunwales
and varnished oars lie across wooden seats
useless as chopsticks on empty plates.

Cots are strung together bow to stern;
moustache-shaped fenders guard prows
against unexpected collisions due to
undertows, or rogue waves slipped

through the harbour mouth by sudden squalls;
the craft are free to ride but not collide.
They roll and yaw on slow insistent waves,
mitigated by piers of Herod's favourite stone.

A separate line of boats face a wall,
bob and nudge each other like drunk uncles
swapping bathroom jokes across urinals,
as if to compensate for a lost pay-day.

Tracing the clinker lines, painted strips
of red and blue converge on jaunty names:
Seaspray II, Tara, Fearless, Lara Sue.
But to-day is laden with absences.

Across the road, in Our Lady's Home,
those in dry dock knit vests and socks
for refugees, gaze out at hollow holds,
empty of fish and loaves and rescued souls.

CLOUDS CEASE DRIFTING

Clouds cease drifting across the sky;
faces frost over and stare into space;
a pendulum resists the lowest point
and still air fails to move the weather vane.

Waves stand frozen in their moulds;
a syringe stays poised over a roped-off vein.
You are all the way down to bedrock,
to the soul's resting place,

with no reserve of energy,
or strength to reach for hope,
only the drone of a chanter
accompanying a slow lament.

Not everything's seized up;
snowflakes float lazily down,
in the vague direction of the street,
gliding sideways, gently as a fall

of apple blossom in late June,
soon accumulating into drifts
of christening lace and candle wax
clustered at the Virgin's feet.

A thaw brings glistening slush,
streaked brown and grey
and life moves on again;
no longer a petrified day.

You move out of the granite niche,
slowly unclenching from the pose.
A searing pain cleaves your head
and leaves you almost blind.

Time resumed can be construed
as warm blood flowing again.

MY CAT'S X-RAY

I don't know what to make
                         of my cat's X-ray.
The first time I saw it
                         I was taken aback
by the solid skull and fangs,
                         the sprung and knotted spine
and the furtive angle formed
                         between femur and fibula.

Where had the cat's cuteness gone,
                         its cinnamon fur, whimsical whiskers,
the button shaped, silent-screen mouth
                         and wide kittenish eyes?
There was nothing to dote over
                         except perhaps the tiny knee caps
and maybe the metatarsals,
                         longer than a hare's hind feet.

But these did not compensate
                         for the whip-like crouching form,
the razored ilium and sacral,
                         the reticulated lizard tail.
Unfortunately, I see through him now;
                         to the raptor behind the fur.
I wonder what an x-ray would
                         show and tell about the inwardness of me.

THE SHAPE OF RAIN

Bruised purple clouds hang around, menacing
as night-club bouncers rubbing their knuckles;
the first drops are ominously large and heavy,
hitting the pavement like squashed sloes.
Smaller drops, riposte in coronets,
join forces as the tempo quickens,
make small magnetic jumps to coalesce
with other blinking eyes of mercury.

The glassy layer floods gutters already
filled by glutted drains; the khaki streams
begin to race; leaves sail by, and paper scraps
and ticket stubs all swept away in confluence,
a regatta of departing souls; the flail
of dancing feet whips up eruptions,
craters and ring-forts, until the hollows over-
flow; then ripples intersect and spread

out into wider gyres and fiddle-heads,
rush wildly down the slope, the pattern
lengthening into the grain of wood—
cell memory, perhaps, of yew and ash.
Marionettes must continue the dance
on small sad feet until the strings break.

MOUSE THROW

The aim was off, and so
the mouse's body landed
in the bough fork of a sycamore tree,
was held there by resinous buds.

The fur was first to go,
thinning to patches of mange;
the flesh turned peat brown
and began to fall away.

Soon there was only a toy
harmonica of bones left
in the tree, the eye sockets
smaller than pin-holes.

Wind could not dislodge
the matchstick structure
because it whistled through
the ribcage with no resistance.

An accidental Indian burial,
the pod remained in place
until an Autumn leaf acted as a sail
and brought the little craft to earth.

FLUKE

Kidneys clean pallid blood
while womb of encased oyster
sighs and pulses with the moon.
A change, when gills suck in seawater
and a particle, unfiltered,
sticks fast in mucus meant to salve.
One grain of sand between shell
and mantle is all it takes to pierce
the heart of our creation goddess.
What can't be spewed must be absorbed;
nacre is secreted layer by layer until
the barb is rounded to conform, a pearl
is made, a planet like a living earth,
formed in the same way by pure chance.

TOUCH

The lioness and I wrestled for most of the afternoon.
I could feel the packed muscles that clenched
Beneath her fur, the rasp of the brawny pitted tongue.
 I drank in her body heat and pounding pulse,
Growls that rumbled upwards from the depths.
Her musk was raw and fuming, redolent
Of sebum, blood salts and stale placenta.
When we fell to lower ground; she broke my fall
And intimacy somehow dulled the impact.
 In the Savannah we rolled over and over,
Locked together, my face against her throat.
She let me feel claws and teeth and the dead weight
Of a club-like paw that could bring down a fleeing
Wildebeest with one casual, almost indifferent, blow.
But I was granted the tolerance she would show
To husky cubs butting against her dugs.

I gripped the rolled flesh of her spine and she forced
My hands open simply by flexing her dorsal muscles;
There were no holds I could maintain without consent.
A lick took some skin off my forehead and a whisker
Grazed my arm; these were accidents but I could feel
A trickle of blood and wondered how she might respond
To its scent. Knowing she could kill me at any second
If she willed it gave our bout a sharp uncertain zest.

There were no antecedents of touch; she would not
Have encountered such a papery hairless hide as mine,
Or the vulnerable body like crabmeat out of its shell.
That may have been to my advantage but who could tell?
The Capricorn sun went lower; other animals watched idly
Then sidled off; there was not enough fresh blood
To make them stay. A jackal came closest and sniffed
Curiously but the lioness growled him away.

This was the purest comprehending of flesh; I had at last
Entered into Nature's heart and met it beat for beat.
As dusk crept across the plain I lay exhausted
In the yellow dust; we were at one and at peace;
She sat nearby on haunches watching me
With twilight calm in her sad unflinching eyes.

A PAIR OF CODGERS

Limber and loose-limbed, the orang-utan came,
pivoting on knuckles, from the back of the cage
to meet me at the plexiglass screen—
only a few centimetres between us
and less than two percent of DNA.

He showed his long incisors and hyena gums
and I displayed my yellow canine stumps,
neither of us overly impressed
or frightened by these phony threats.
Miserable wisps of orange hair sprouted
from his leathery, oak-tanned hide.
Miserable strands of grey streeled
across my crumpled parchment head.

He had a habit of drawing a cupped hand
all the way from cranium to chin,
dejected by everything around him,
all the empty chatter of visitors;
sometimes he would just hold his head,
as if to fend off a bout of migraine,
and use his hands as blinkers to screen out
all the pointless activity round about.

No wild man he, but more the sad old man
of the jungle where I had soldiered too;
we were a pair of codgers who needed time
to come to terms with past travails,
misdeeds—of which a multitude.
He sat, legs buckled; I crouched in mime,
unable to accept the offered chunk of orange;
we were still eye to eye through the glass,
familiar cameos reflected in the brown
pupils which hinted at defeated strength,
and fading recall of better times;
he may once have played and wrestled
with clinging young as I had done.

All different now, said the wise old face,
ineffably sad, lugubrious in its deepest folds,
knowing the game was up, of that no doubt.
He was; he stayed; this cage would see him out.

FEELING THE ECLIPSE

The street slows as the annulus glows;
then inevitably that moment of perfect
coincidence beyond imagining or prophesy.

Despite the thin halo of light, darkness falls:
a chill descends, mist or miasma,
birds perch in silence, and we stand stock still,
ash-coloured ghosts, fretful and alone,
frozen in the dull tideway light,
caught between stasis and flight.

Dumbstruck, we gaze, prone again to fate,
insignificant among marvels, perfectly
aligned in an unruly universe.
Who could dare believe that this sequence
of elements and events merely happened?

THE CORMORANT FISHING COMPANY

On a still lake ringed by karst mountains
the fisherman stands in his blue boat
and smooths the cormorant's wing feathers.

He calms the bird as he passes a noose
of silken thread over her gleaming head,
then pays out the line; when she catches

a fish, he tugs the cord to prevent swallowing
and to bring the bird back to his boat; he adds
the fish to the growing pile in the stern.

He urges the cormorant to dive in again;
by evening when dusk darkens the blue,
the fisherman rewards the bird with a few

sprats which she is allowed swallow.
At least I'm not starving, the bird thinks,
and this Master isn't the worst, but still

I'd like to be able to fish for myself;
I've heard of places beyond the mountains
where you can swallow whenever you like.

THE TRINITY CAT

The Trinity cat pads out of his laurel bush
at 9 on the dot. A ginger tom with upright tail,
he loiters at the library scanning the crush
of commuters most recently arrived by rail

who take a short-cut through the campus,
until he spies the one with liverwurst
in grease-proof paper in her purse.
He starts towards her, diffidently at first,

then at a trot, makes obeisance at her feet
(though really brands her with his scent),
rises to the patting hand, smells the meat
and lets himself be led to a pavement

where a manhole cover serves as a dish
on which she decants his breakfast;
he hunkers down and sniffs; it's not fish
but will do in a pinch. Food at last!

His rhythmic chews are measured and deft;
he tosses back his head to swallow,
doesn't look up or notice she's left;
he'll see her from his laurel bush to-morrow.

ANOTHER PRESENCE

In the clearing of a sitka wood,
a vixen briefly stands to taste
the August air with tapering snout.
Mildly curious she yawns and blinks
and eyes me for a while,
then follows at a distance,

dawdling, coming close at times
then veering off in coils and loops
around the path I take.
The clever black eyes—fine-drawn
punctuation marks smudged back—
look sad in her thin face.

The russet coat is matted
with mud and pine needles;
a ruff of lighter fur under the chin
and the meagre, threadbare tail
are marks of advancing age.
Spindle-shanks dwindle down

to clumped blackberry paws.
The joints seem stiff and brittle;
several litters have taken a toll;
she does not have many summers left.
A magpie swoops from a branch
of spruce to pick at her fur.

I wave it away and for an instant
the vixen lets me pat her head,
perhaps to conjure up some food
as in that Aesop fable we all read.

MR. PHOTON

Dressed in a shiny suit, carrying a neat
white case, he steps down from the plane.
A band on the runway strikes up;
he is not overly impressed by the forced
harmonies—so unlike those that accompanied him
on his long sojourn in the vanguard,
through the myriad spheres of ordered space,
galaxies, supernovae, red giants fusing gold.
He expected better from this entropic planet—
the latest stop on his long-haul itinerary.

Over lunch the Mayor adorns him
with garlands of platitudes.
In his reply Mr. Photon is a little rude—
the wave part of his nature takes over
from the more stable particle side.
He reminds them that he is the first light
of his star to reach this pathetic planet,
and that his star has just expired.

The Mayor sympathises with Mr. Photon;
he himself is an orphan and knows
the pain of separation and a world without colour.
Mr. Photon is about to apologise
when he turns grey and slowly fades away.

NOSTOS

i.m. John Moriarty, Poet and Mystic

Back from the Cretan maze,
without help from winding thread,
you recognised the coastline
that never really let you go,
and remembered how:
Kevin raised nestlings
in outstretched hands,
an obliging fly marked the page
in Colman's book, and kept
him awake to finish the text,
Brigid's cows gave extra milk
to keep her visitors refreshed,
a hedgehog lapped up the precious ink
that Ruadhán spilled, and let
his spikes be used as quills
until the gospel was complete.

When your hair began to thin
you left strands on the window sill
for birds who whisked away
the interlaced coils of thread
for weaving silver nests.

THE CLIMBER THINKS OF HOME

On a ledge of cliff, between sea and sky,
he sees below the sweep of bay, scooped
sand dunes, jellyfish like wet brains,
razor shells for sambas, and all the manes
and knots of seaweed strewn on rocks.

Memories of home blurred by vertigo:
bare feet sucked by shifting sand
and undertow, salt in teeth and eyes,
jinking sand flies like specks of soot,
landing on the pages of his comic-book.

Nor can he forget Helen's warming breath,
her small teeth nibbling water melon,
and the indignant wood of confessionals,
nor that first visit to the casualty ward
smelling of ether, polish and bib dribble.

An image of the kitchen: the tumbling
rhythm of butter churn, issuing
irate gander hisses of pent-up gasses,
the glass port-hole with clouds that cleared
when the first smudge of curds appeared.

In the lower field flocks of sheep
grazed slowly with soft, shuttling lips.
Close to the wood, unsettled deer
began to prance in fear, ready
to flee from the half-witted dog.

Clinging to the sheerest face,
a femur fractured in two places, he fears
the lure of sleep and tries to find
familiar hand-holds from the past.

SANDMAN'S LULLABY

Through the window I saw
our youngest son at the piano
playing Sandman's Lullaby.

In shorts and runners his feet
dangled from the bench
unable to reach the pedals.

He was playing the whole piece
not practising; his face in repose
in grainy shadow of October sun.

The melody drifted on the haze,
the notes discovered slowly,
sometimes a little late.

Not wanting to intrude, I waited
at the gate; in a year or two
he would take up football

but not yet, and for the moment
it was a marvel. O, it was an air,
a tuneful air he made.

WAITING WITH A VIEW OF THE LANE

He didn't want to be met at the airport
So she waited at the gate, open to the lane,
Hedged with speckled holly, yellow sedge.
At some point he would appear round the bend
Of the lower field; she would see his easy gait
And first spreading smile of recognition.

The sky was hoarse with crows, and from
The lane a lazy heat haze rose; a long-footed
Hare crossed to the other hedge and disappeared;
Full-blown summer here, so he would have left
The Australian winter on the other side.
How that unstuffy, life-breathing land

Must have suited him down to the ground.
Phone-calls were short, he was always rushing
To scuba dive or paraglide, and had swum
In all the magnificence of the barrier reef.
At any second he could appear, framed between
The holly tree, and hanging bough of fuchsia.

As he came closer she would begin to see
His features blend into the expression
She had missed for an entire year.
She sat on the wall by the gate pier and kept
In view the bend at the end of the lane.
She wanted that first image to file away;

Her wandering son did not return every day.
There would be a saunter, a bag slung over
A shoulder, that dawning smile and brown face;
There would be the familiar expression
Slowly forming as he came closer...

The sun went down and dusk crawled up the lane.

GOING HOME THAT NOVEMBER

One of the last suns of autumn
gives the city a wistful glow.
Fretted shadows of elm trees
bridge the water at intervals;
a boat keel leaves a chevron wash
and passing birds land on narrow

feet, scoring the glass of the canal.
On the tow path are ghosts of friends
sauntering at will among the trees.
Where are they now and where
the witless fun that probably
served some purpose after all?

They may abide in havens overseas,
trawling the dwindling hours God sends;
there are memories too of Kavanagh,
the purification that calmed his spirit
and raised it to the wing-nest of a swan,
gliding into mist towards Helicon.

I fear the burden of misplaced pretence
and hope she will be resigned
yet somehow spared the truth
in her declining winter months.
The coach drops me near the door
which yields to a fingertip.

A MANDOLIN HUNG IN THE SHED

Stored in a shed near the stable,
bottled cure-alls for cattle
on a lame table, harnesses,
horse brasses, bee-hives.
A mandolin hung in the shed.

In a corner old sacks last used
on bent knees for beet drills,
rock salt, sheep shears, paint spills,
and a butter churn long discarded.
A mandolin hung in the shed.

Startling to light on this find,
ethereal in cobwebs and dust,
an object so delicately made
it ached for a satin-lined case.
A mandolin hung in the shed.

Sweets of sin in a wineskin,
it could fill cupped hands
snugly, right up to the brim
though fragile as eggshell.
A mandolin hung in the shed.

The outer skin peeled in strips
shaped like eucalyptus leaves;
mellow walnut, and inlay
of maple to charm the dead.
A mandolin hung in the shed.

At your touch a spider ran out
of the gourd and pinged off a string,
a hint of latency that lay within;
the carapace warmed to your hand.
A mandolin hung in the shed.

A curved ladle to draw from a well's
hollow depth, your father must have
played it, might even have made it
right there in the shed.
A mandolin hung in your head.

A PLANE AT NIGHT

From a distance overhead
the umber drone of a plane
somewhere in dense black night,
a ghostly siren echoing
in the background of our minds,
though no bombs will fall to-night.
Unaided by moon or stars
I find wing lights in the sky;
those on board are going away,
always going, not coming back,
not always strangers either, and I can
imagine two souls by a port-hole,
trying to find me in dark spaces
among scattered city lights.

RECOGNITION

A standard class photo taken in the 20s,
Monochrome, with white fold lines,
Fly-blows and bottle rings, shows:

Boys in three terraced rows
Against a long white-washed wall
With paint-flaked sash windows.

A black cat lies snoozing in the yard;
Nearby, teachers' bikes lean against a wall.
Too informal for a First Communion Day,

What the occasion was is hard to say;
Maybe the photographer just happened
By the village that sleeping afternoon,

An hour that disappeared too soon
And would have been forgotten
Had the camera not snapped it up.

Bowl-cuts and sticky-out ears abound,
Wrinkled collars loosened for neck boils;
A class of fifty, few smiles to be found,

Mostly men's grimaces after hawking phlegm,
Or pinched squints on sun-blind faces.
Who are they and what became of them?

In the front row with socks rolled down
To scuffed and dusty boots, a sturdy boy
Sits with hands on knees but does not frown.

The sun soft-feathers his features;
Face quizzical, not dour; eyes clear.
Of all the places I've searched
I never imagined he would be here.

JUST MARBLES

The big glassies could skid on flag-stones
or skip over the line of downers.
Sometimes a worn ball-bearing, pitted
with flaws like pater noster lakes, could make
a better shooter, more ponderous, and likely
to knock a few majolicas or pearlies
out past the chalk circle's perimeter.

An alternative was to grind a handful
of glassies together in a pocket
until they formed craters of their own;
the added traction could control
excited urges to bobby-dazzle and be slick.
Glassies had swirls of colour deep inside
like fossils in amber—clusters of coral,
yellow and red, floating in a clear lagoon.

The shooter had to feel right in the palm
when rolled and cocked to fire between
knuckle of thumb and tip of finger;
as the flint-lock pressure slowly built,
the ratchet slipped and the shooter
catapulted out in a spurt of colour,
spinning up the surface of the path

to blend with iridescent blues and purples
of downers sent flying from the circle,
comets shooting through galaxies,
in streams of scintillating hues.
Losses tragic: sparklers in another's pocket;
wins magic: new coral depths to ponder,
though never fathom—for in those lanes
we were bred on mysteries.

WATER PLAY

When we dammed up streams
with rocks and clay we could see
limpid water deepen, dimple
in willow green behind the weir;

we never doubted that water was alive;
it never ceased to seek out
avenues of escape, around or through
impacted mud that could absorb no more.

And the stream's curious intelligence
could always finagle out a runnel
or hidden culvert to serve its purpose,
and reclaim its chosen path.

We watched channels and gullies
being formed by cleveralities
with quick-witted speed,
could predict when outlets

would be discovered in a flash,
silver tines rake out crumbs
of earth from the barrow's core
and the flow resume its course.

As keepers of the lock we might
play God, draw a finger through
wadded mud and wait for the new
groove to be flooded in an instant.

The stream did not always need to find
the line of least resistance; it could breach
the dam and wash chunks of tumulus away,
showing how frail solidity could be.

Because of sun on water we were
often golden blind and forced to rest
on sloping banks to get our vision back.
But even then we could tell by sudden

rushing sounds when weaknesses were found.
We beavered in those elements on summer days
and saw how water dealt with hindrances
to find and follow its own way.

THE STILL CENTRE

It was necessary to tie the right
number of knots in the tail of the whip
so that the string would engage
the spinning top just enough,
allegro ma non troppo.
A surfeit of knots could cause

tangles, hoist the top into the air
and sling it dangerously anywhere.
With the right, caressing wield of lash
the top would dance on its ferule,
the colours of the carousel
tending to a whirling blend of white.

It could be nursed along
by deft touches of the flail
without bias to the purl
which paralleled the spindle
of the world, even when the top leapt
up and spun in its own vortex of air.

On the ground it would sing,
then hum, its colours blurring
into one; it would go to sleep and live
within itself, dead to the world.

ANCIENT ENTERTAINMENT

Marrakesh, circled by Atlas mountains;
at its heart a square, Djemma El-Fna,
framed by Medina and Mosque,

and small dusty, half-deserted shops
which do not seem to have a purpose yet.
Merchants in Djellabas shout, *Over here,
for souvenirs! Cheaper than Souk!*

When sun loses the glare of noon
drums, castanets and Berber flutes begin;
stall-holders display silks and carpets,
spices, dried fruits; fragrant smoke issues

from Tagine pots and flaming grills.
The space slowly yields to crowds;
rough-hewn men with biblical faces
bearded and baked in desert kilns,

bear down on those who venture close.
Yellow lights come on at evening,
and the square brightens to a stage
for thimble-rigging and plate-spinning;

snake charmers fill their chanters
with sounds of flustered pterodactyls;
clusters of fakirs vie with rope walkers,
belly-dancers, oil-soaked fire-eaters,

water carriers with brass bells, canteens
of goatskin, wizard hats and motley
of mirage red—an oasis where caravans
and tribesmen come for entertainment,

real as antiquity, untouched by TV
or hippies who once passed through.
The clay-hard men are out of place
on this lantern-lit stage because levity
denies the truer burden of their lives.

A FATE TAKES A HOLIDAY

Lost to landscapes scrolling past,
She sits knitting in the carriage of a train;
The blurred needles scintillate and glance
To the upbeat cadence of the wheels.

Rows of tiny coils and eyelets like beads
Of condensation, gather on the upper rim
As she zips along with loops and riffs,
Nimbly delving with needle tips,
Her tilted face serene and still.

Once in a while she gives a heave
To loosen more yarn from the skein
Of Curragh wool—brushed worsted weave,
Spun and carded from the richest fleece—
Deep in the wicker basket by her feet.
With each tug the feeding line of yarn
Becomes less taut and life flows on
More easily in these kind reprieves.

The needles flash mesmerically
With ancient rhythms and attack
Of duellists in their chain-mail coats.
With little hesitation she can tack
From plain to purl to blackberry,
Count back by rote or slip a stitch
While the fish-eyed gimlets gleam.

The rib-worked cables fall and teem
From her enthralling hands;
Tresses and plaits, braided fields
Of heraldry, Celtic-cross evangelists
With smocks and little saintly feet
All gather profusely in her lap,
As windfall trove, rich-patterned

And warm with peach-fuzz nap,
All crafted from a single line of yarn.
Marvels fall continuously from wise
Spell-binding hands and all is well for now.

GOLD OR GRAIL

Despite the zanies and idolators,
there were many who believed
that this strange blend of science
and religion could succeed
if the Philosopher's Stone
could be conjured or conceived.

According to ancient texts, the correct
alkahest consisted of highly rectified
spirits of wine, mercury, a minim of
aquafortis, and essence of emery.
Adepts were enslaved by kings and nobles
hungry for gold, the sinews of war.

When the hermetic scientists rested
from their labours they were expected
to amuse the court by casting nativities.
Was it naïve to trust that God
and reason could achieve mutation?
Was it not the essence of hope

that gold was there, in potens, waiting
to be brought forth, as a human form
waits for a sculptor in a block of stone,
as the Lord of all waits in bread?
For some the prize was gold itself;
others wanted to be blessed by the act,

to be singled out for ordination.
All were obsessed by the moment of discovery,
and entire lives were devoted to imagining
not an apparition or manifestation,
but that sublime fraction of a second
when they might see creation.

THE HORSEMAN DREAM

The horseman is first seen
On a distant ridge just above
The horizon. The image seems
Flat against the sky, deprived
Of depth and movement.

He fades momentarily,
Descending the grey shoulder
Of the hill, then emerges faintly
Against background rocks,
Not much more than a blur though
Surprisingly closer than before.

Shade your eyes against the sun;
Details appear, a glancing sheen
On the horse's flanks, puffs of dust
From hooves, suggesting speed.
The rider's face is still unseen
But direction is all too clear.

Look again: no idle canter this;
The double-headed image
Is approaching at a gallop,
Through fresh-turned furrows
Of scattered sand and scree,
With purpose and fidelity.

Now on the level plain
You see, with dawning fear,
The rider rise and fall,
Vaguely in a molten haze;
A spectre shimmering
To an ancient rhythm of attack.

A SPLINTER OF LIGHT

Unlike migrating birds
we have no destination
and our journeys are broken
well before completion.

Though resurrection
is a hopeful tale
it turns on aspiration;
reason judges it of no avail.

The superlative gift
will be reclaimed in time.
Enlightenment and love,
all we have learned in a lifetime
will be irrecoverably lost.

An animal's eye holds no fear
but we know it is a stone's throw
from Eden to Gethsemene.
We watch our cell mates go down
the passage-way one by one

and though we try to disbelieve
that someday it will be our turn to leave,
we wonder when our hour will come
to end what we are and could become.

We have no choice coming in
and none going out....save one.

FASHION (or Zeitgeist?)

Avoidance is our only measure of worth.
Painters must steer clear of deepest hues;
burnt sienna, alizarin crimson, cobalt blues
are all de trop, while sunsets and seascapes
are deemed too operatic by far.

A modest metaphor might be construed
as safe, but similes carry health warnings
and other tropes must be eschewed.
One slip into excess is all it takes
to curdle the whole into a mess.

Passion is incontinence; we are
embarrassed by it. Bones only,
no flesh or soft tissue allowed.
Less is more. We fear intensity
and true meaning's density.

Last century saw rituals and rallies
that shattered enlightenment;
better to avoid than commit,
unless we learn new passions.

COMA

What complex journey brought you
to intensive care? A fall from sun,
a forced landing from those high
regions you explored, more likely

a sea voyage that fell foul
of sudden squalls and storms?
The ventilator rises and falls,
a piper chanting your life

to a weakened pulse-beat,
and tubes and intravenous lines
keep you tied and trammelled,
you who travelled every continent

of map and mind, now hopelessly
entangled. These are not your life-lines;
you have been inveigled into this snare.
Cast off all ties, bow and stern;

weigh anchor, put out to sea again
and clear the harbour wall by sunset.

SUCH CLOSENESS

Taking a break from his labour
Ed sits by the headstone, unwraps
his lunch—a beef sandwich and a pear.
Nearby, a shallow stream mirrors
stands of yew and cypress trees
moving vaguely in the breeze.

After lunch he resumes his work,
wire-brushes lichen off the cross
and the grave's surrounding stonework.
Then he uses a hoe to remove the moss
sprouting through the marble gravel;
he redefines the inscription with a chisel.

With Cemetery Sunday just ahead
it is incumbent on family members
to show respect for their dead
at the ceremony of remembrance.
Joe Carroll arrives late at a half-trot,
begins sprucing up his neighbouring plot.

'You have yours shining like a jewel',
he says, beginning to scour and spray.
My God, Ed thinks, we sat together at school,
drilled in the FCA, brought in each other's hay,
delivered calves, went to the same confraternity,
and we'll be cheek by jowl for all eternity.

I WAS A FROZEN EMBRYO

My parents did the deed outside the womb
and I am the fruit or living proof.
I waited for three years on the third shelf
while my folks kept their options open and
the fridge door shut. When they got the SUV
and detached house they decided
to implant me back into the womb
and the rest is my-story. A close call though;

If they'd shilly-shallied much longer
I'd have passed my shelf life, been junked,
incinerated or had my stem cells harvested.
Anyway, I'm here now, so let's go on
with our lives, as they say, one of which
I happen to have. Who is really wanted anyway?
Did your folks know it would turn out to be you,
You?

RICHLY IMPRESSIVE THEN

Little girls in white lace
bear baskets of flowers,
scatter petals along the nave
for concelebrating priests
to walk on in basalt shoes

as they process with slow
rolling gait to the altar,
their faces round and pink,
joined hands like puffin beaks
propped on stomachs.

They smile proprietorially
to pews both left and right,
while one dips and shakes
the aspergillum to douse
the flock with holy dew.

At the back, on bony knees
your senses fill with incense,
radii of candle-light and flare
of sanctuary lamp striking
tabernacle gold, as your soul
strives with tangles of ritual.

BROKEN CIRCLE

No circle is true to the ideal;
even fairy forts are flawed;
let us not imprison
or exclude but leave
a little gap for visitants.

Knowledge is incomplete;
we need an opening that
a spark can leap across,
from where imagination can sally
forth to other worlds and breathe.

A harbour welcomes ships
and allows more civil wind usher them
safely to their moorings.
A caret signals what is missing
for conception to occur.

There is no perfect rounded soul;
the space left empty fires us up.
Do not rush to close the gap
with rubble or capstone; see it
as a door, left open to welcome
any gods who may pass by.

LEAVENED BREAD

Black pestles pound all night as the mix
of gluten, flour and autolyse heaves,
subsides and heaves again; bakers slowly
excavate slabs of dough for final moulding.
They knead the impressionable stuff,
stretch it to effacement and back again
to more solid strata, tuck in the flaccid
fuse, up and over, fold in all loose ends

with barm and yeast, sprinkle yet more flour.
They cut it into chunks to fit the moulds,
loaf, duck and bloat, pack it in—just enough
cargo in each boat—slice off extraneous
flaps and tags; Procrustean knives give final
signature cuts which in heat will open
like gargoyle mouths as yeast pushes up white
tongues through the crust before it hardens.

Ovens are bellowed up to furnace heat,
moulds slide in on wooden peels, doors bolted.
Dough winces and darkens quickly in the
low-roofed chambers. The ghostly bakers
sit and wait for the shape-shifting dough
to settle on the purity of inner form.
Sweat traces pink runnels in white masks
as the *bauernbrot* nears completion.

TOLSTOY'S MYRIAD LANDSCAPES

At Yasnaya Polyana the avenue lined
with silver birch curved from the white
mansion past the sheds where serfs bore,
in their gathered smocks, freshly-cut
resinous logs for loading on sleds.

The avenue led to the Voronka river
where he walked with Aunt Tatiana
to see cranes rise from reeds,
straighten to the shapes of spears
and brave snow-flurried skies.

His brother told of a green stick
which bore a carved inscription
in answer to a deep inquiry;
it was hidden in the forest bordering
the Moscow-Kharkov railway-line.

Diary entry: To be or do, feel or think?

He saw a wretched prisoner guillotined
in Place de la Roquette, and knew
that men were irretrievably corrupt,
yet perfection haunted him ceaselessly
as he lurched between sins of flesh and pride.

Then back to flaying remorse
until the sweet panic of lust rose again.
What gall to challenge me to a duel,
when he refused to acknowledge
the son he had with Aksinya!

Being merely what he was, despite
self-mastery, he substituted rules
and causes for people, landscapes
for feelings, and—to his wife's shame—
belated and infrangible chastity for love.

Diary entry: Nothing done, no salvation.

He tried to wrest truth from God's embrace,
and find the green stick at the station
near the tracks where Anna fell to death,
by that forest place he always sought—
even at Sevastopol—but never found.

SNAPSHOT AND WAFFLES

In the gilt and scarlet foyer,
behind the Agatha Christie aspidistras,
there hangs a framed photograph,
black and white, and speckled:
Conseil de Physique Solvay,
Bruxelles 1911, Hotel Metropole.

Elderly men with troped moustaches,
heavy suits and fob watches, stare gravely.
Planck, Rutherford and Solvay positively glare.
In front, seated, is Marie Curie, side-face
resting in slender palm, engrossed
in some learned paper being shown to her

by the stooping figure of Poincaré.
The century is young and there is
still time for enlightenment to lift
the veil from the face of Isis.
At right, standing, is the young Einstein,
a cigarette butt cupped in his hand,

the way a corner boy would try
to shield a lighted tip from the wind.
He's about twenty-eight or nine.
The handsome face is more or less
impassive. An effort has been made
to comb out the tangles of black hair.

With head craned forward, he looks
faintly ill-at-ease in this company.
Do they regard him as an upstart,
however promising and smart?
Is he wondering how he might escape
these bookish ancients for a while

and have some waffles in the sunlight?
Does he realise how it will be
three years from now, how the skies
will darken in his lifetime, and how,
despite its constancy, the light will die?

WHERE IS THE GUIDE?

When the wolf swallowed the sun
and the jewels of light were
scattered wide when Lucifer fell
there was every reason to fear.

Now at the crossroads between Delphi
and Thebes—the ford no easier—
we tremble in fright as the snake spits
out bad figs and swallows its tail.

All auguries fail; bird flight tells us
nothing, nor leaves in the wind,
and we must accept that base metal
will not leap to a fifth essence.

Virgins no longer wake pregnant
and smiling under the almond tree;
the veil of Isis is not raised, and blood
has lost redemptive power.

Mandrake growing from the semen
of hanged men is our only fruit.
The day of atonement has passed
as we twist and turn without a star.

GIVERNY AND OTHER GARDENS

Pulsing limes and lindens, aspens,
tresses of willow cascade down
to choreic water; the crushed light
stunned by irises, agapanthus,
clefted lily pads troped as palettes.
At the centre, a curved bridge
formally centres the elements
under swags of ivy and clematis,
almost completes a circumflex
in reflecting water; wooden baulks
give solidity and rootedness
to varied wilderness, the span
a metaphor for echoes that pass
between Eden and Gethsemene.

GUITAR IN SHOP WINDOW, CAMDEN STREET, 2017

Resting on its side, full-bodied and calm
as the reclining Buddha, the rounded wood,
inlaid with mother-of-pearl around
the Aeolian mouth, endows the space
inside with such rich imagined echoes
you can hear a tortoiseshell plectrum
being drawn across the strings as fingers
of infinite finesse dance up and down
the star-spaced frets, and feel the drowsy grace
of Andalucian homes, whiter than sunlight,
ascending hills, their stucco balconies
facing out to sea, through drapes of jasmine,
looking down on fields of sunflowers, olive groves,
wineskins hanging in the shade of trees.

ENGLISH SPEAKS SEDUCTIVELY

I place a trove of word signs freely
at your feet as would a good genie;
use me. I am biddable, and aim to please;
not frozen in time I gladly embrace
each day new words and idioms;
in me you can explain yourself more easily;
grow with me. *Clasp my hand and come.*

I allow more distinctions of meaning;
can sieve and re-combine the tiniest grains;
I can be tragic or amusing, innocent, risqué,
and can reflect your mood swings to a tee,
can even hint at what you meant to say
or, for hidden reasons, left unsaid.
The threat of deconstruction is a fib
and doesn't frighten me; my text is stable.

You may experiment with me; I permit
fluency, confidence, persuasion, wit,
discussion of dreams and consciousness
in streams; express your heart's desire in me.
My pedigree is interesting though not inbred
and I have spawned offspring in foreign parts:
Creole, Pidgin, Franglais, biblical tongues.
I am diamond-cut beyond your dreams.

I've fed on the best roots and truffles
from classics of the Med to Courtly French;
I can be clear, ambiguous—imagist if you wish.
I could have helped extol your cattle
and malting barley, apply for lower rent,
cosy up to the powers that be, those who
inherited me. You could have risen in society.

Don't count on fanatics to revive
your own poor tongue; I knew
and loved her well. They'll turn her into
a grotesque changeling you never knew.
Grant her the dignity of a good burial.
I am the market place of laissez parler;
there are no boundaries to be seen;
join me now in my court of universal
dreams. I am what you mean.

ARBONAUTS IN A GONDOLA

Arbonauts in a wicker gondola
balloon over the Amazon rain-forest,
studying the life-filled canopy
that has reached closest to the sun,
observing the moon-eyed bush babies

that live in this green penthouse.
By modulating fuel and rudder they can
sail and tack among the tree-tops,
fully in control, unlike poor Sweeney
who wept and fell more than he flew.

The balloon saves them from climbing
trees with complex ropes and harnesses,
coping with spiders on the forest floor,
side-winding snakes, wild monkeys and macaws.
They like working from the top down,

with a reserve of academic distance,
safe from chafing, and stings of killer bees.
From that comfortable height do they see
too much forest and not enough trees?

BRISE-SOLEIL

Galileo had observed that the blurs of light
in the Milky Way were composed of stars,
not smears expressed from Hera's breasts.
He had seen the moons of Jupiter,
Saturn's rings, magnificent flares of fire
leaping from the sun's perimeter.

Milton had imagined other worlds,
born of epic wonder and belief,
but had also witnessed marvels,
and gave much value to the outer eye,
before it failed him utterly, sometimes
empowered by telescope—
the Tuscan artist's optic glass.

Both were blind when they met in Arcetri.
It would have been Milton who insisted
that myths of melting wings, earth-falls
and the compensation of clairvoyance
for sight, did not apply to them.
Galileo would have reluctantly agreed:
they were fortunate to have understood
in God's good light what they had once seen.

LOVE POEM

If you were sawn in half your cross-section
would show neat layers of tissue and skin,
a thin stratum of sweet fat,
legended by colour and pattern,
and organs like acorns in their cups,
sectioned kidneys in transparent cauls,
healthy pink hollows of lung, the heart
enthroned alone in its scarlet hall,
bones with marrow eyes, nested in
porcelain ball-and-socket joints,
tensile tendons and sinews
binding up the package neatly like
a Valentine gift; *your* beauty is not skin deep.

SWIMMING TO ICELAND

I'm swimming to Iceland
to see volcanic moon acne,
new islands, life beginning,
to hear whales playing
alto clarinets in the dark.
I'm swimming to Iceland
to see my friend Gisli,
his sons and *dottirs*,
their backyard *geysirs*
and long-boats on fire.

I'm swimming to Iceland
to see lava fields of sheep,
sturdy little Viking horses
trotting by while golden plovers
sing away winter snows.
I'm swimming to Iceland
to gather eider-duck down
from nests to warm the eggs
of guillemots and arctic terns
before they fly to the south pole.

I'm swimming to Iceland
to find the purity of ice
and fire, and to drink water
of melting glaciers, filtered
through pores of pumice.
I'm swimming to Iceland
because I have a layer
of blubber, oak-tanned hide,
lungs of many verses
and a goose-greased soul.

When swimming to Iceland
I will mostly do the crawl

and may, if lucky, grab
a passing dolphin's tail.
I may turn on my back
while swimming to Iceland
and let a flying fish sit
on my belly as a sail.

Monks once threw away
their oars to find the grail.

I KNOW THE SCORE

Oh, she was guilty all right,
caught red-handed in the act
by many reputable witnesses,
leading citizens to a man,
all in good standing with the law.

I would normally have led off
but on that day I hesitated.
The faint-hearted who hoped
to follow my lead in safety
as they usually do, mocked me,

and spurred me on. *The law
must be obeyed*, they cried.
Do not fail in your duty.
But I somehow knew this
was not a day like other days.

I knew by his eyes that he knew;
no question in his mind or mine.
No need for a special sign to show
that he saw right through me;
but to leave me in no doubt

he bent and wrote in the clay
near where the red-haired woman
lay; he wrote several names and mine
appeared at the head of the list.

No, I wasn't going to be the first
that day, or the last on any day.
I stayed my hand and walked away.
I do not have the gift of a soothsayer
or the quick wit of a temple trader
but I know when I haven't got a prayer.

BACK TO THE WORLD

It was the custom in the Middle Kingdom
that when a man or Mandarin was dishonoured
by the State and had no right of appeal,
he would quietly leave his home
and sit on a riverbank, shore of sea
or lake, with unbaited fishing line.

He would gaze into the water and watch
the contour of the unavailing line
trailing idly in the waves,
his back turned to the world.
Passers-by would see the rounded back,
know he had been wronged in some way,

and that a man's protest in those times
could be no more than the helpless
gesture of a slighted child.
They would hurry past, eyes downcast,
and he would not turn in case he might
embarrass or include them in his plight.

ALWAYS IN SEARCH

He stoops and turns over
layers of seaweed with his stick,
strops of bladderwort and dulse,
as salt water soaks his thin shoes.
A grey heron on a rock deems him
harmless and resumes its vigil of a pool;
it unloops a long neck to stab the water.
What gifts of tide this morning of grace?

The sea is a sheet of silk, lifting slightly
on a breeze, its magic hidden below
the surface, though sometimes glimpsed
in the tear-stained eyes of seals.
In wetlands he combs through reeds,
disturbs wading birds and swans
with their young. A cob flies at him;
the white cyclone scares him away.

Between Thebes and Tara he watches
turnstones search for grubs in heavy soil
hungry for burials; he envies the birds'
instincts and moves on, using the stick
to knock seed heads from poppies,
purple thistles and wild flowers;
he lifts swathes of drying hay—still
green underneath—roots in hedges,

enlivens in vain the crumbling
deadwood, bran-chaff of last year's
dying back; old nests in bough-forks
disintegrate in ancient dust.
Among hills he seeks the source
of rivers, beneath likely outcrops,
rummages through serrated forests
of Sitka spruce for the holy well.

Scraw and cottontails are torn from bogs,
as he digs down through dark layers
of peat to black oak and tanned bones.
Not close enough; he turns elsewhere,
feels the pulse of peeled hazel
and the tug which marks the source.
But he cannot settle for spring water
or any find bound to earth.

Acknowledgements

THE LOSS THAT HEIGHT ENTAILS	Shortlisted for Strokestown Poetry Award, 2002
A FATE TAKES A HOLIDAY	Winner Atlanta Review Prize 2003, *Atlanta Review*, 2003, Anthologised in the *Gift of Experience*, Summer 2005
STILL CENTRE	Winner, Writers Week Listowel Volume, 2000
SEEING WATER	Winner, Siarsceal Poetry Award, Castlerea, 2008
A MANDOLIN HUNG IN THE SHED	*Envoi*, No 134, Feb 2003
ANOTHER PRESENCE	Ibid
A SPLINTER OF LIGHT	*Poetry Ireland Review*, No 72, 2002
GEOLOGISTS	Ibid
SANDMAN'S LULLABY	*Poetry Ireland Review*, No 54, 1997
BACK TO THE WORLD	Ibid
TOUCH	Ibid
GIVERNEY AND OTHER GARDENS	Shortlisted for the Writers Week Listowel Prize
A PAIR OF CODGERS	Shortlisted for the Tonbridge Wells Award, 2007
JUST MARBLES	Shortlisted for the Clogh Award, 2005
ALCHEMY	Shortlisted for the Clogh Award, 2006
BULLOCH HARBOUR	Prizewinner in the Gregory O'Donoghue Competition, Shortlisted in Golden Pen Competition, St Kerrill's Journal, 2009
SUCH CLOSENESS	Ibid
LEAVENED BREAD	Highly Commended, Boyle Poetry Festival Awards, 2009
CLOUDS CEASE DRIFTING	*Revival*, 2010
FLIGHT	Winner, the Georgia Poetry Society Award 2003. Anthologised in the GPS Anniversary Collection
THE CORMORANT FISHING COMPANY	*Cyphers*, 2010
GOING HOME THAT NOVEMBER	*Cyphers*, 2012
TOLSTOY'S MYRIAD LANDSCAPES	*Poetry Ireland Review*, 2012
THE HORSEMAN DREAM	*Abridged*, 2013
GUITAR IN SHOP WINDOW	*Atlanta Review*, Spring/Summer, 2013
LOVE POEM	*Atlanta Review*, Spring/Summer, 2013
SNAPSHOT AND WAFFLES	*Orbis*, 2014
THE SEA'S UNCERTAINTY	Highly Commended, Siarsceal Festival, 2012
ALWAYS IN SEARCH	Goldsmith Poetry Award, 2015
ENGLISH SPEAKS SEDUCTIVELY	High Commendation, Hungry Hill, 2015
BIRDS OF SALT AIR	*Allegro Poetry Magazine*, March 2019
MOUSE THROW	*Southword Poetry Journal*, Munster Literature, 2017
THE CLIMBER THINKS OF HOME	Highly Commended, The Francis Ledwidge International Poetry Award, 2015
WAITING WITH A VIEW OF THE LANE	Commended, Ibid. 2018
FLUKE	*Humanagerie Anthology*, 2018

MICHAEL G. CASEY, an Irish National, married with three children, was educated at New Ross, University College Dublin and at the University of Cambridge where he earned a Ph.D. He has worked and taught in Dublin, Cambridge, Washington DC and the Caribbean Islands. His poetry and short fiction have appeared in many Irish, British and American journals. Winner of several national and international awards, he has been anthologised with writers such as Seamus Heaney, Nadine Gordimer, Derek Walcott, Billy Collins, and Jorge Luis Borges. He has published novels and a prize-winning collection of short fiction (2007). A book, entitled *Ireland's Malaise* was published by the Liffey Press in October 2010. Nine of his stage plays (short and full-length) have been produced by the Umbrella Theatre Company, one, by invitation, in the Henrik Ibsen Museum, Oslo. He has written for *The Irish Times* and *Sunday Times*. Although he has published numerous individual poems in various journals, *Broken Circle*, is his first collection.

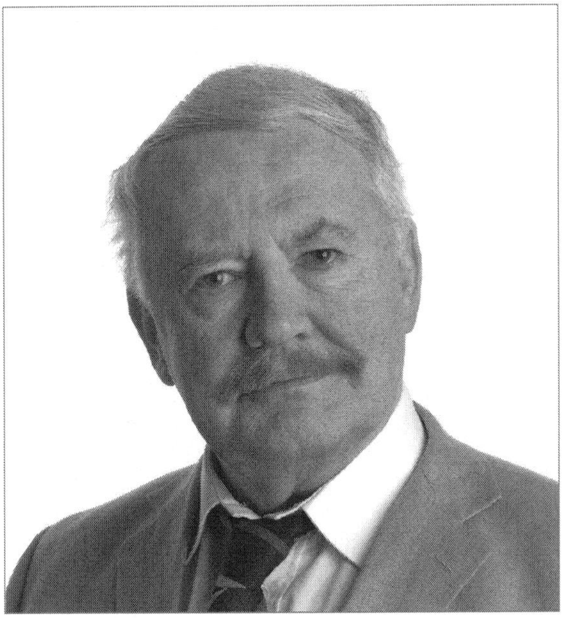

salmonpoetry

Cliffs of Moher, County Clare, Ireland

"Publishing the finest Irish and international literature."
Michael D. Higgins, President of Ireland